Bridging Faith and Mental Health

Equipping Ministry Leaders for Informed, Faith-Centered Mental Health Responses

Dr. Giovanna L. Sanders, Ed.D.

Dedication

This manual is dedicated to the ministry leader.
Healthy pastoral care is strengthened through connection, accountability, and continued learning.
You are not called to walk this journey alone.

ISBN: 979-8-9945199-0-5

Published by Crowned Warrior Publishing

United States of America

First Edition

DISCLAIMER

This publication is intended for educational and training purposes only. It is not a substitute for professional mental health diagnosis, treatment, or legal counsel. The author and publisher do not provide clinical, medical, or legal services. Clergy and ministry leaders are encouraged to work within the scope of their training and to collaborate with licensed mental health professionals and appropriate authorities when necessary.

Contents

Introduction

Clergy serve on the front lines of emotional, spiritual, and relational care. In today's complex and rapidly changing society, pastors and ministry leaders are increasingly encountering congregants who are navigating mental health challenges alongside matters of faith. While clergy are often trusted as first points of contact, many report feeling underprepared to discern appropriate responses, boundaries, and next steps.

Bridging Faith and Mental Health was developed to equip clergy with practical tools, foundational knowledge, and a clear framework for responding to mental health concerns within a pastoral context. This training recognizes the sacred role of clergy while also acknowledging the limits of pastoral care and the importance of collaboration with mental health professionals.

This program focuses on building awareness, reducing stigma, and strengthening a clergy member's ability to create safe, supportive spaces for conversation, discernment, and referral. Participants will explore key concepts related to mental health, pastoral responsibility, ethical considerations, and effective intervention strategies that honor both spiritual formation and emotional well-being.

This training manual is a curated compilation of lessons, frameworks, and practical tools developed through teaching, ministry experience, and engagement with clergy at various stages of formation. While designed to function as a stand-alone resource, it may also be used in conjunction with the companion book, ***Navigating the Maze of Mental Health and Ministry***. This additional resource detailing the seven phase ***Clergy Mental Health Referral Process*™** can be used by clergy seeking a more in-depth, structured framework focused specifically on the referral process. Together or independently, these materials are intended to strengthen discernment, support ethical pastoral care, and encourage sustainable ministry rooted in both wisdom and soul care.

How to Use This Manual

This training manual is designed to be used in a variety of settings, including self-paced study, group training, and facilitator-led instruction. Each section builds upon the previous one, offering both conceptual understanding and practical application. Reflection questions, discussion prompts, and case-based examples are included to encourage thoughtful engagement and real-world integration.

Key terms used throughout this manual are defined in the **Glossary** located at the end of this guide.

Training Overview

This training program is designed to increase mental health literacy among clergy by providing foundational knowledge, practical skills, and ethical guidance for responding to mental health concerns within a pastoral context. The following overview outlines the core components of the training and how each section builds upon the next.

Training Modules at a Glance

Module 1: Introduction to Mental Health
Module 2: Recognizing Common Mental Health Conditions
Module 3: Faith and Mental Health
Module 4: Communication Skills and Pastoral Boundaries
Module 5: Pastoral Discernment and Referral
Module 6: Crisis Awareness and Immediate Response
Module 7: Clergy Self-Care, Burnout, and Sustainability
Module 8: Cultural Awareness and Sensitivity in Mental Health Care
Module 9: Legal and Ethical Considerations in Pastoral Mental Health Care
Module 10: Evaluation and Participant Feedback
Module 11: Follow-Up Support and Peer Collaboration

Module 1: Introduction to Mental Health

Module Overview

Clergy often serve as trusted first points of contact for individuals experiencing emotional, psychological, or spiritual distress. As mental health concerns become more visible within congregations, pastors and ministry leaders are increasingly called upon to respond with compassion, wisdom, and discernment. This module provides a foundational understanding of mental health and mental illness within a pastoral context, equipping clergy with shared language and awareness while maintaining appropriate professional and ethical boundaries.

This module is not intended to prepare clergy to diagnose or treat mental health conditions. Instead, it establishes essential knowledge that supports informed pastoral care, early recognition of concern, and timely referral when additional support is needed.

Learning Objectives

By the end of this module, participants will be able to:

- Define mental health and explain its importance to overall well-being
- Distinguish between mental health and mental illness
- Identify broad categories of common mental health conditions encountered in ministry
- Recognize general signs and symptoms that may indicate emotional or psychological distress
- Understand why mental health literacy is essential for effective pastoral care

Understanding Mental Health

Mental health refers to an individual's emotional, psychological, and social well-being. It influences how people think, feel, act, relate to others, handle stress, and make decisions. Mental health is not static; it can change over time and is shaped by life circumstances, relationships, physical health, and support systems.

For clergy, understanding mental health is essential because it affects how congregants experience faith, relationships, crisis, and daily life. Emotional distress does not exist apart from spiritual life, and spiritual struggles do not occur in isolation from emotional well-being. A foundational understanding of mental health allows pastors to respond with clarity, compassion, and appropriate care.

Mental Health vs. Mental Illness

Mental health and mental illness are related but distinct concepts. Mental health reflects a general state of well-being, while mental illness refers to diagnosable conditions that significantly affect mood, thinking, behavior, or functioning.

Mental health exists on a continuum. Individuals may experience periods of stability, distress, or impairment depending on life circumstances, stressors, and available support. Mental illness represents one end of that continuum and may require professional intervention. Recognizing this distinction helps clergy avoid minimizing distress while also avoiding premature conclusions or diagnoses.

Overview of Common Mental Health Conditions

Clergy may encounter a wide range of mental health concerns within their congregations. While diagnosis is outside the pastoral role, familiarity with common categories can support informed and compassionate responses. These may include:

- **Mood disorders**, such as depression and bipolar disorder
- **Anxiety disorders**, including generalized anxiety disorder, panic disorder, social anxiety disorder, and post-traumatic stress disorder (PTSD)
- **Psychotic disorders**, such as schizophrenia
- **Personality disorders**, which may affect emotional regulation and interpersonal relationships
- **Substance use disorders**, which often co-occur with other mental health challenges

This overview is intended to promote awareness, not assessment. Understanding these categories helps clergy recognize when additional support may be needed.

Recognizing Signs and Symptoms

Mental health concerns often present through changes rather than isolated events. Clergy should be attentive to shifts in behavior, mood, thinking, or daily functioning. Common indicators may include persistent sadness, heightened anxiety, withdrawal from relationships, confusion, changes in sleep or appetite, emotional volatility, or expressions of hopelessness.

Recognition does not require certainty. It requires attentiveness. Noticing patterns and changes allows clergy to offer support, ask thoughtful questions, and determine appropriate next steps without assuming clinical responsibility.

In ministry settings, these changes may surface gradually and are often shared indirectly through prayer requests, relational conflict, declining participation, or expressions of spiritual struggle.

Clergy are frequently positioned to notice these shifts because of ongoing relational proximity rather than formal assessment. Recognizing signs and symptoms, therefore, is less about identifying a diagnosis and more about discerning when something is "off" and deserves gentle attention. This awareness helps clergy respond early, before distress escalates or becomes a crisis, while maintaining appropriate pastoral boundaries.

In many ministry contexts, early indicators of emotional distress surface at the altar, often framed as prayer requests rather than explicit expressions of mental health concern. Individuals may request prayer for "peace," "clarity," "strength," or "rest," while underlying symptoms such as anxiety, depression, grief, or trauma remain unspoken. Because altar moments are spiritually charged and emotionally vulnerable, congregants may feel safer naming spiritual language than articulating emotional pain. Clergy attentiveness during these moments is especially important, as repeated or escalating altar requests can signal deeper distress that warrants follow-up beyond the public moment of prayer.

The altar should be understood not only as a place of spiritual encounter, but also as a space where emotional burdens surface indirectly. While prayer remains essential, clergy benefit from recognizing when an altar response may be the beginning of a larger pastoral conversation rather than the conclusion of one. Thoughtful follow-up—offered privately and without assumption—allows prayer to remain sacred while also opening pathways for additional support when needed.

Why Mental Health Literacy Matters for Clergy

Mental health literacy strengthens a clergy member's ability to respond with confidence, compassion, and appropriate boundaries. When pastors understand mental health at a foundational level, they are better equipped to create safe spaces for conversation, reduce stigma within faith communities, and guide congregants toward additional resources when needed.

Healthy pastoral care does not replace professional mental health treatment. Instead, it complements it by offering spiritual support, presence, and discernment while recognizing when collaboration with mental health professionals is necessary.

Mental health literacy refers to the knowledge and understanding that support the recognition, management, and appropriate response to mental health concerns. Mental health literacy encompasses not only awareness of mental health conditions, but also the ability to access information, reduce stigma, and make informed decisions about care and support. Within ministry settings, this literacy is not about becoming a clinician, but about developing informed awareness that supports ethical, compassionate, and effective pastoral leadership.

At a foundational level, mental health literacy for clergy includes:

- Understanding common mental health concerns and how they may present in everyday life and ministry contexts
- Recognizing early signs and patterns of emotional distress

- Knowing when concerns fall within the scope of pastoral care and when referral is appropriate
- Reducing stigma by normalizing conversations about emotional and mental well-being
- Being aware of available resources and referral pathways within the community

When clergy develop mental health literacy in these areas, they are better equipped to respond thoughtfully rather than reactively. This knowledge supports healthier boundaries, reduces the pressure to "fix" complex issues, and strengthens collaboration between spiritual care and mental health support. Ultimately, mental health literacy allows clergy to serve with greater confidence, clarity, and care for both congregants and themselves.

Without basic mental health literacy, clergy may feel uncertain, overwhelmed, or pressured to address concerns beyond their training. Increased understanding allows leaders to normalize emotional struggles without minimizing spiritual formation or faith practices. It also supports ethical decision-making by helping clergy recognize when continued pastoral care is appropriate and when referral is in the best interest of the congregant. Over time, this literacy contributes to healthier ministry cultures where emotional well-being and spiritual growth are not viewed as competing priorities.

Module 1 Reflection

Before moving forward, take a few moments to reflect and record your thoughts.

How have mental health concerns shown up in your ministry context?

Where do you feel confident responding, and where do you feel uncertain?

How might increased mental health literacy support healthier pastoral boundaries?

Section Review

Before continuing, reflect on your learning in this section.

What information in this section was familiar or already known to you?

What new information or insights did you gain from this section?

The next module builds upon this foundation by exploring how common mental health conditions may present within ministry settings.

Module 2: Recognizing Common Mental Health Conditions

Module Overview

Clergy are often among the first to notice changes in a congregant's emotional state, behavior, or engagement. This module focuses on recognizing common mental health conditions as they may present within ministry settings. Emphasis is placed on observation, pattern recognition, and pastoral discernment rather than diagnosis or treatment. Participants will learn how to notice when distress is persistent, escalating, or interfering with daily functioning and spiritual life.

Learning Objectives

By the end of this module, participants will be able to:

- Identify common mental health conditions frequently encountered in ministry contexts
- Recognize behavioral, emotional, and relational patterns associated with these conditions
- Distinguish between temporary distress and ongoing mental health concerns
- Respond with appropriate pastoral care while maintaining professional boundaries

Depression

In ministry settings, depression often presents as more than sadness. Clergy may notice persistent low mood, loss of interest in activities once enjoyed, fatigue, withdrawal from relationships or church involvement, and expressions of hopelessness or worthlessness. Spiritual language may include feelings of abandonment by God or loss of purpose. When these patterns persist over time or intensify, additional support may be needed.

Anxiety Disorders

Anxiety may present through excessive worry, restlessness, irritability, difficulty concentrating, or physical symptoms such as tension or sleep disturbance. Congregants may frequently seek reassurance, express fear about the future, or struggle to find peace despite spiritual practices. Anxiety becomes concerning when it consistently interferes with daily functioning, relationships, or spiritual engagement.

Trauma and Post-Traumatic Stress

Trauma-related concerns may emerge following experiences such as abuse, violence, loss, or disaster. Clergy may notice heightened vigilance, emotional numbness, avoidance of reminders, intrusive memories, or sudden emotional reactions. Spiritual struggles may include questions about safety, trust, or God's presence. Trauma responses often fluctuate and may intensify around anniversaries or reminders.

Substance Use Concerns

Substance use may surface through changes in behavior, mood instability, impaired judgment, secrecy, or relational conflict. Clergy may observe increasing dependence on substances to cope with stress, emotional pain, or trauma. Substance use often coexists with other mental health challenges and may require coordinated support beyond pastoral care alone.

Psychotic Symptoms

While less common, psychotic symptoms may include disorganized thinking, delusional beliefs, hallucinations, or significant detachment from reality. Spiritual content may become intertwined with symptoms, making discernment challenging. When these signs are present, immediate professional evaluation is typically necessary.

Patterns, Duration, and Impact

Recognition involves more than isolated behaviors. Clergy should consider patterns over time, duration of symptoms, and impact on functioning. Persistent distress, escalating symptoms, or impairment in relationships, work, or spiritual life may signal the need for additional intervention or referral.

Pastoral Role in Recognition

The pastoral role in recognition is to notice, listen, and respond with care—not to diagnose or treat. Healthy recognition supports compassionate conversation, appropriate boundaries, and timely referral when needed. Awareness allows clergy to remain present while ensuring congregants receive the level of care they require.

Module 2 Reflection

Before moving forward, take a few moments to reflect and record your thoughts.

Which patterns are you most likely to notice first in your ministry context?

How do you currently discern between temporary distress and ongoing concern?

What helps you remain attentive without feeling responsible to "fix" the problem?

Section Review

Before continuing, reflect on your learning in this section.

What information in this section was familiar or already known to you?

What new information or insights did you gain from this section?

The next module explores how faith and spiritual beliefs can shape the way mental health is understood, experienced, and supported within ministry contexts.

Module 3: Faith and Mental Health

Module Overview

Faith plays a significant role in how individuals understand suffering, healing, hope, and meaning. For many congregants, spiritual beliefs serve as a source of strength and resilience during emotional distress. At the same time, faith can sometimes complicate mental health experiences through guilt, shame, misunderstanding, or spiritual pressure. This module explores the intersection of faith and mental health, equipping clergy to navigate both the supportive and challenging aspects of spirituality with wisdom and care.

Learning Objectives

By the end of this module, participants will be able to:

- Describe how faith can positively and negatively influence mental health
- Recognize spiritual struggles that may accompany emotional distress
- Identify common faith-based misconceptions related to mental health
- Support congregants in integrating spiritual care with mental health support
- Navigate ethical tensions between faith beliefs and evidence-based care

The Relationship Between Faith and Mental Health

Faith often shapes how individuals interpret pain, resilience, healing, and identity. Spiritual beliefs may offer comfort, community, and purpose, while also influencing how mental health concerns are understood and expressed. Recognizing this relationship allows clergy to respond with sensitivity rather than assumption.

For many individuals, faith provides the primary framework through which emotional experiences are processed. Language of prayer, spiritual warfare, calling, or obedience may be used to describe anxiety, depression, or trauma without those terms ever being named. Clergy awareness of this interpretive lens helps leaders listen more carefully for what is being communicated beneath spiritual language.

Understanding the relationship between faith and mental health also helps clergy avoid false dichotomies. Emotional distress does not negate spiritual maturity, nor does strong faith eliminate vulnerability. When clergy acknowledge that faith and mental health are interconnected rather than opposed, they create space for honest conversation and more effective pastoral care.

Positive Impacts of Faith on Mental Health

Faith can serve as a powerful source of coping and support. Prayer, worship, community, and shared belief can reduce isolation, foster hope, and provide meaning during difficult seasons. Religious communities often function as vital support systems that promote emotional resilience.

Spiritual practices can help individuals regulate emotion, strengthen identity, and maintain perspective during times of stress. Rituals, sacred texts, and communal worship often provide grounding and continuity when life feels unstable. For many, faith offers a narrative of hope that sustains them through prolonged difficulty.

Faith communities also provide relational support that extends beyond formal care. Fellowship, service, and shared spiritual life can counter loneliness and create a sense of belonging. When these elements are present, they can significantly support emotional well-being and recovery.

Spiritual Struggles and Religious Stress

Not all spiritual experiences are comforting. Congregants may struggle with doubts, unanswered prayers, guilt, or fear of spiritual failure. Religious expectations or teachings may unintentionally intensify shame or discourage seeking help. Clergy must be attentive to these dynamics and respond with compassion rather than correction.

Spiritual struggle is often deeply personal and may be accompanied by silence or withdrawal. Individuals may fear that expressing doubt or emotional pain will be interpreted as weakness or lack of faith. This can lead to internalized pressure to appear spiritually "strong" while suffering privately.

Clergy responses during these moments are critical. When leaders normalize spiritual struggle as part of the faith journey, they reduce shame and invite honesty. Compassionate listening allows congregants to explore their questions without fear of judgment or dismissal.

Guilt, Shame, and Misconceptions

Faith-based misunderstandings about mental health—such as viewing distress as a lack of faith or moral failure—can prevent individuals from seeking help. Addressing these misconceptions is essential for reducing stigma and promoting holistic care.

Messages that unintentionally link suffering to sin, disobedience, or insufficient prayer can deepen shame and discourage disclosure. Individuals may internalize these beliefs and delay seeking support until distress becomes severe. Clergy awareness of these dynamics helps interrupt harmful narratives.

Teaching that affirms both spiritual formation and emotional health allows congregants to seek help without fear. When leaders model balanced language around suffering and healing, they create a culture where asking for support is seen as wisdom rather than failure.

For individuals serving in roles where the preservation of life may also involve the taking of life—such as military service, law enforcement, or other protective occupations—experiences of guilt and shame may be uniquely complex. Actions taken in the course of duty, even when lawful and intended to protect others, can conflict deeply with personal faith convictions, moral values, and spiritual identity. These internal conflicts are often carried silently and may surface indirectly through spiritual language, emotional withdrawal, or persistent feelings of unworthiness.

In these cases, shame is not rooted in moral failure, but in moral injury—the distress that arises when individuals are forced to act in ways that collide with deeply held beliefs about life, justice, and righteousness. Clergy pastoral care must resist simplistic explanations or theological shortcuts. Instead, care requires careful listening, theological humility, and space for lament, confession, and meaning-making. When clergy acknowledge the moral weight of these experiences without judgment, they create room for healing, reconciliation, and appropriate support to unfold over time.

Religious Coping Practices

Spiritual practices such as prayer, meditation, ritual, and communal worship can support emotional well-being when used appropriately. Clergy play a key role in encouraging healthy spiritual practices while recognizing when additional support is needed.

Healthy religious coping supports reflection, connection, and resilience. Practices that invite rest, community, and honest expression can be particularly beneficial during seasons of emotional strain. When used flexibly, spiritual disciplines can support both spiritual growth and emotional regulation.

However, spiritual practices should not be used to suppress emotion or avoid addressing distress. Clergy discernment is needed to recognize when practices are serving as support and when they may be functioning as avoidance. Encouraging balance helps ensure that spiritual life remains life-giving rather than burdensome.

Ethical Tensions and Pastoral Discernment

Clergy may encounter ethical tension when faith beliefs intersect with mental health care. Respecting spiritual convictions while supporting evidence-based treatment requires discernment, humility, and collaboration. Healthy integration honors both spiritual care and professional boundaries.

Some congregants may resist mental health care due to fear, stigma, or theological concern. Clergy must navigate these conversations carefully, honoring belief systems without reinforcing harmful misconceptions. Ethical pastoral care involves supporting informed decision-making rather than persuasion or pressure.

Discernment also includes recognizing the limits of pastoral expertise. Collaboration with mental health professionals allows clergy to remain spiritually present while ensuring congregants receive appropriate care. This partnership strengthens trust and protects both the congregant and the clergy member.

Cultural and Denominational Considerations

Faith traditions vary widely in how mental health is understood and addressed. Cultural background and denominational teaching influence beliefs about suffering, healing, and help-seeking. Clergy must remain culturally and theologically sensitive in their responses.

Cultural norms may shape how emotions are expressed, whether distress is shared publicly or privately, and how authority figures are approached. Awareness of these factors helps clergy avoid misinterpretation and respond more effectively to congregants' needs.

Denominational teachings may also influence expectations around prayer, deliverance, or endurance. Clergy who understand their own theological context—and how it is heard by congregants—are better positioned to offer care that is both faithful and responsible.

Creating Supportive Faith Communities

Faith communities can play a vital role in supporting mental health through education, openness, and compassion. Clergy leadership sets the tone for whether mental health concerns are met with understanding or silence.

When leaders speak openly about emotional health, it signals permission for others to do the same. Teaching, preaching, and programming that acknowledge mental health concerns help normalize these conversations and reduce stigma.

Supportive faith communities do not replace professional care but reinforce it. By fostering environments of safety, connection, and understanding, congregations become spaces where individuals feel supported in both their spiritual and emotional journeys.

Module 3 Reflection

Before moving forward, take a few moments to reflect and record your thoughts.

How have you seen faith support healing in your ministry context?

Where have spiritual beliefs complicated mental health care?

How can your leadership foster both faithfulness and emotional health?

Section Review

Before continuing, reflect on your learning in this section.

What information in this section was familiar or already known to you?

What new information or insights did you gain from this section?

The next module focuses on developing effective communication skills that help clergy listen, respond, and support individuals navigating mental health challenges with empathy and appropriate boundaries.

Module 4: Communication Skills and Pastoral Boundaries

Module Overview

Effective pastoral care begins with effective communication. When congregants share mental health struggles, the way clergy listen and respond can either foster safety and trust or unintentionally cause harm. This module focuses on developing empathetic, attentive, and ethical communication skills that support healing conversations while maintaining appropriate pastoral boundaries.

Learning Objectives

By the end of this module, participants will be able to:

- Demonstrate active listening skills in pastoral conversations
- Respond with empathy and validation without judgment or assumption
- Use open-ended questions to encourage meaningful dialogue
- Recognize the role of non-verbal communication in supportive presence
- Maintain healthy pastoral boundaries while offering care

Active Listening in Pastoral Care

Active listening involves giving full attention to the speaker, seeking understanding rather than solutions, and communicating presence through words and posture. Techniques such as paraphrasing, reflecting feelings, and summarizing help congregants feel heard and respected.

Active listening requires intentional slowing down. In ministry settings, clergy are often approached with urgency, expectation, or emotional intensity, which can create pressure to respond quickly. Practicing active listening helps shift the focus from problem-solving to presence, allowing congregants to feel genuinely seen and understood.

This type of listening communicates care without overstepping pastoral boundaries. By reflecting what is heard rather than offering immediate advice, clergy create space for congregants to clarify their own thoughts and emotions. Over time, this approach builds trust and encourages deeper, more honest conversations.

Empathy and Validation

Empathy allows clergy to connect emotionally without absorbing or fixing another person's pain. Validation communicates that a person's experience matters, even when solutions are not immediately available. Empathetic responses focus on understanding rather than correction.

Empathy does not require agreement or endorsement of every perspective shared. Instead, it involves recognizing the emotional reality of the person speaking. Statements that acknowledge pain, confusion, or fear help congregants feel less alone in their experience.

Validation is especially important when individuals feel misunderstood or dismissed elsewhere. When clergy validate emotions without minimizing or spiritualizing distress, they reinforce that emotional expression is not a failure of faith. This approach fosters safety and supports ongoing pastoral engagement.

Empathy is not agreement, endorsement, or emotional overidentification. It does not require clergy to take on another person's pain, choose sides, or suspend discernment. Empathy also does not mean rescuing, fixing, or resolving distress on behalf of the congregant. Instead, it involves understanding and acknowledging emotional experience while remaining grounded, objective, and appropriately distanced. This distinction allows clergy to offer genuine care without becoming overwhelmed or crossing ethical boundaries.

Using Open-Ended Questions

Open-ended questions invite deeper reflection and sharing. Rather than directing the conversation, these questions allow congregants to express their experiences in their own words. Thoughtful questioning supports insight while avoiding interrogation or assumption.

Effective open-ended questions are curious rather than corrective. They invite exploration without steering the conversation toward predetermined conclusions. This allows congregants to name what feels most important to them rather than responding to what they think clergy want to hear.

Clergy should remain attentive to pacing and tone when asking questions. Too many questions at once can feel overwhelming, while well-timed questions can gently deepen understanding. Discernment helps ensure that questions serve the person, not the process.

Examples of Open-Ended Questions in Pastoral Conversations

Open-ended questions invite reflection rather than closure and allow congregants to shape the conversation in their own words. The following examples illustrate questions that encourage exploration without pressure, assumption, or direction:

- "Can you tell me more about what this has been like for you?"
- "What feels most difficult about this situation right now?"
- "When you think about what's been happening, what stands out to you?"
- "How has this been affecting you day to day?"
- "What have you noticed about how this has changed your relationships or routines?"
- "What does support look like for you in this season?"

These types of questions communicate curiosity rather than correction. They help congregants slow down, reflect, and articulate experiences that may not yet be fully formed. Used thoughtfully, open-ended questions deepen understanding while preserving the congregant's agency and sense of safety.

Encouraging Deeper Sharing When Responses Are Limited

Some congregants struggle to articulate their experiences and may respond with one-word answers or brief statements such as "fine," "okay," or "I don't know." These responses often reflect emotional overwhelm, fear, exhaustion, or uncertainty rather than resistance. In these moments, the goal is not to pressure disclosure, but to gently invite further sharing at a pace that feels safe.

Clergy can support deeper sharing by normalizing the difficulty of putting feelings into words and by offering prompts that expand the conversation without interrogation. Simple follow-up statements often communicate patience and presence more effectively than additional questions.

Examples of gentle prompts that encourage elaboration include:

- "Can you help me understand what 'fine' looks like for you right now?"
- "When you say 'okay,' what does that mean in this situation?"
- "Would you like to tell me a little more about that?"
- "What made you choose that word?"
- "Sometimes it's hard to find the words—take your time."

Reflective statements can also open space without requiring immediate answers:

- "It sounds like this has been weighing on you."
- "I notice you paused there—what's coming up for you?"
- "I'm here with you; there's no rush."

These approaches communicate safety rather than urgency. By remaining patient and curious, clergy allow congregants to share as they are able, when they are ready. Over time, this gentle posture often leads to greater trust and deeper conversation.

Non-Verbal Communication

Non-verbal cues such as eye contact, posture, facial expression, and tone of voice significantly shape how messages are received. Clergy should be mindful of their own non-verbal communication to ensure it conveys attentiveness, calm, and respect.

Congregants often interpret non-verbal signals more strongly than spoken words. Distractions, hurried posture, or guarded expressions may unintentionally communicate disinterest or discomfort. Awareness of body language helps reinforce verbal messages of care and presence.

Non-verbal communication also plays a role in emotional regulation. Calm posture and steady tone can help de-escalate intense emotions. Clergy who remain grounded physically often help others feel safer emotionally.

Responding to Emotional Distress

Emotional expression may include tears, anger, fear, or silence. Clergy are called to remain grounded and present during intense moments. Responding with calm reassurance, patience, and compassion helps regulate the emotional tone of the conversation.

Emotional distress can be uncomfortable to witness, especially when clergy feel unsure how to respond. The goal is not to stop emotional expression, but to remain steady within it. Silence, when offered attentively, can be as supportive as words.

Clergy responses during emotional moments set the tone for future disclosure. When individuals experience acceptance rather than urgency to resolve distress, they are more likely to return for continued support. Presence communicates safety when answers are not yet clear.

Supporting Without Fixing

Pastoral care does not require having answers or solutions. Attempting to "fix" emotional pain can shut down honest expression. Supportive presence focuses on walking alongside rather than taking control of the situation.

Fixing often emerges from discomfort rather than care. When clergy rush to provide solutions, it may unintentionally communicate that emotions are problems to be eliminated. Supportive presence allows space for processing without pressure.

Walking alongside means honoring the congregant's agency. Clergy support reflection, discernment, and next steps without assuming responsibility for outcomes. This approach protects both the congregant's growth and the clergy member's sustainability.

Maintaining Pastoral Boundaries

Healthy boundaries protect both clergy and congregants. Maintaining appropriate limits ensures that care remains ethical, sustainable, and effective. Boundaries help clergy remain supportive without assuming responsibilities beyond their role.

Boundaries clarify expectations around availability, confidentiality, and scope of care. Without clear boundaries, clergy risk emotional exhaustion, role confusion, or dependency dynamics. Healthy limits allow pastoral care to remain consistent and trustworthy.

Maintaining boundaries also models healthy relational practices. When clergy demonstrate appropriate limits, they normalize balance and self-care for congregants. Boundaries are not barriers to care; they are structures that support it.

Boundaries can be understood as informed responses shaped by observed patterns rather than emotional reactions or moral failure. Over time, individuals teach us—through behavior, consistency, urgency, or disregard for limits—how they will engage when given access to our time, energy, and availability. Boundaries are not punishments or withdrawals of care; they are decisions made based on the data people provide about what they need, what they expect, and how they respond when limits are present.

For clergy, this perspective is especially important because guilt often replaces discernment. Many leaders feel compelled to remain endlessly available, believing that faithfulness requires constant accessibility. When boundaries are framed as abandonment rather than stewardship, clergy may override their own limits in the name of care. Burnout often lives in this space—not because clergy care too much, but because they ignore the information they have already been given about what is sustainable.

Burnout is a state of emotional, physical, and spiritual exhaustion that develops when sustained demands consistently exceed available capacity and support. In ministry, burnout often emerges gradually through chronic overextension, blurred boundaries, and the internal pressure to remain endlessly available. It is not a sign of weakness, lack of calling, or insufficient faith, but a predictable outcome when limits are ignored or overridden for extended periods. Burnout will be explored more fully in **Module 7**, where clergy self-care, sustainability, and long-term ministry health are addressed in greater depth.

Healthy pastoral boundaries acknowledge reality without resentment. They recognize that clergy cannot be everything to everyone, and that presence must be paced to remain effective. By responding thoughtfully to what behavior has revealed—rather than to pressure, urgency, or fear—clergy protect both their calling and their capacity. Boundaries, when informed by discernment, allow care to continue over time instead of collapsing under exhaustion.

Confidentiality and Ethical Awareness

Confidentiality is foundational to trust in pastoral relationships. Clergy must understand when confidentiality applies and when safety or legal considerations require additional action. Clear communication about limits of confidentiality supports transparency and integrity.

Ethical awareness helps clergy navigate complex situations responsibly. Congregants are more likely to share openly when they understand how information will be handled. Clear explanation of boundaries around confidentiality prevents misunderstanding and protects trust.

Clergy must also remain informed about mandatory reporting and referral obligations. Knowing when confidentiality must be broken for safety ensures that care remains both compassionate and lawful. Ethical clarity strengthens pastoral credibility.

In many ministry settings, clergy may also choose—though it is not always required—to include another trusted individual in pastoral conversations when meeting with congregants of the opposite gender. This practice is intended to provide accountability, clarity, and protection for both the clergy member and the congregant. When this approach is used, it should be communicated openly and respectfully in advance, ensuring that the congregant understands who will be present and why. Transparency around this practice supports trust, reinforces ethical boundaries, and helps prevent misunderstanding or discomfort during pastoral care encounters.

Follow-Up and Continued Support

Pastoral conversations do not always end with resolution. Thoughtful follow-up communicates care and consistency while reinforcing boundaries. Ongoing support may include prayer, check-ins, or referrals when appropriate.

Follow-up signals that the conversation mattered and was not forgotten. Even brief check-ins can reinforce connection without creating dependency. Consistency builds trust over time and encourages continued engagement.

Ongoing support should remain intentional and appropriately paced. Clergy discern when follow-up is helpful and when referral or additional resources are needed. This balanced approach sustains care while honoring pastoral limits.

Practice Scenario: Active Listening vs. Not Listening

A congregant, Taylor, comes to you feeling overwhelmed by ongoing financial stress and uncertainty. Taylor expresses anxiety about meeting basic needs and feels embarrassed asking for help.

Consider the following:

- What cues indicate Taylor needs to feel heard rather than fixed?
- How would active listening shape your response in this moment?
- What types of responses might unintentionally shut the conversation down?
- How can empathy and open-ended questions support further dialogue?

This scenario may be used for group discussion or individual reflection.

Module 4 Reflection

Before moving forward, take a few moments to reflect and record your thoughts.

How do you typically respond when someone shares emotional pain?

Where do you feel most confident in listening, and where do you struggle?

What boundaries help you remain present without becoming overwhelmed?

Section Review

Before continuing, reflect on your learning in this section.

What information in this section was familiar or already known to you?

What new information or insights did you gain from this section?

The next module addresses pastoral discernment and referral practices, helping clergy determine when additional professional support is needed and how to navigate that process with care and confidence.

Module 5: Pastoral Discernment and Referral

Module Overview

Clergy are often entrusted with deeply personal and emotionally complex concerns. While pastoral care plays a vital role in spiritual and emotional support, there are times when professional mental health intervention is necessary. This module equips clergy to discern when referral is appropriate, how to communicate that decision with care, and how to continue offering pastoral support without exceeding professional boundaries.

Learning Objectives

By the end of this module, participants will be able to:

- Understand the scope and limits of the pastoral role in mental health care
- Recognize indicators that suggest the need for referral
- Communicate referral decisions with compassion and clarity
- Provide appropriate resources and support during the referral process
- Maintain ethical boundaries while continuing pastoral care

Understanding the Scope of the Pastoral Role

Clergy provide spiritual guidance, emotional presence, and pastoral support, but they are not trained mental health clinicians. Recognizing the limits of one's role protects both the congregant and the clergy member. Healthy pastoral care includes knowing when additional expertise is needed.

Clarifying the scope of the pastoral role helps prevent role confusion and unrealistic expectations. Congregants may look to clergy for answers, direction, or solutions that exceed pastoral training. Naming the boundaries of the role early allows clergy to offer care with confidence rather than hesitation.

Understanding scope also protects the integrity of pastoral ministry. When clergy remain grounded in their role as spiritual caregivers rather than informal therapists, they model ethical leadership. This clarity supports sustainable ministry and reinforces trust within the congregation.

Building Trust and Clarifying Confidentiality

Trust is foundational to pastoral relationships. Clergy should communicate confidentiality clearly, including its limits related to safety or legal obligations. Transparency supports trust and prepares congregants for next steps when referrals become necessary.

Clear communication about confidentiality reduces fear and misunderstanding. Congregants are more likely to share openly when they understand how information will be handled and when it may need to be shared for safety. Addressing confidentiality early prevents feelings of betrayal later.

Clarifying confidentiality also supports ethical decision-making. When expectations are clearly established, clergy are better positioned to act responsibly if concerns escalate. Transparency strengthens the pastoral relationship by reinforcing honesty and integrity.

Indicators That Suggest the Need for Referral

Referral may be appropriate when:

- Emotional distress is persistent or escalating
- Functioning in daily life is significantly impaired
- Symptoms suggest serious mental health concerns
- Substance use interferes with health or relationships
- Progress does not occur despite pastoral support

Recognition is not diagnosis, but it does inform responsible action.

These indicators help clergy discern when pastoral care alone may no longer be sufficient. Referral decisions are based on patterns, duration, and impact—not on isolated moments of struggle. Paying attention to these signs allows clergy to act proactively rather than reactively.

Referral is a responsible pastoral response, not an admission of inadequacy. Recognizing when additional support is needed reflects care for the whole person. Early referral can prevent worsening distress and supports more effective long-term outcomes.

Engaging in Referral Conversations

Referral conversations should be direct, compassionate, and collaborative. Asking clear questions and normalizing professional support helps reduce fear and stigma. Framing referral as an extension of care—not a failure—supports acceptance.

Many congregants experience anxiety or shame when referrals are introduced. Clergy can ease this by using calm, respectful language and emphasizing shared goals for well-being. Collaborative conversation reinforces dignity and choice.

Approaching referral without urgency or pressure allows congregants time to process. When clergy remain present and supportive, referral becomes a bridge rather than a rupture in the relationship. This approach strengthens trust even during difficult conversations.

Providing Resources and Facilitating Connection

Clergy can assist by providing contact information for mental health professionals, support services, or community resources. When appropriate, helping initiate contact can reduce barriers to care while respecting autonomy.

When providing referrals, clergy benefit from thoughtfully vetting mental health providers before sharing their information. Vetting does not require evaluating clinical competence, but it does involve ensuring that providers are appropriately licensed, operate within ethical standards, and are accessible to the populations being served. Simple steps such as confirming licensure, areas of specialization, and accepted insurance plans help clergy offer responsible referrals without assuming clinical oversight.

Clergy may also consider how well a provider understands or respects the role of faith in a congregant's life. While mental health professionals are not required to share a congregant's beliefs, it can be helpful to identify providers who are open to integrating spiritual considerations when appropriate or who demonstrate cultural and religious sensitivity. Asking general questions—such as whether a provider has experience working with faith-informed clients—can help ensure referrals align with congregants' values without imposing expectations.

Maintaining a small, diverse referral list allows clergy to offer options while avoiding endorsement of a single provider. Referral lists should be reviewed periodically and updated as availability, credentials, or community needs change. Clergy should remain clear that inclusion on a referral list does not imply responsibility for treatment outcomes. By vetting thoughtfully and referring transparently, clergy support congregants in accessing care while preserving ethical boundaries and pastoral integrity.

Follow-Up and Continued Pastoral Support

Referral does not end the pastoral relationship. Thoughtful follow-up communicates care and reinforces support while maintaining boundaries. Clergy remain a spiritual presence even when professional care is involved.

Follow-up reassures congregants that they have not been abandoned. Simple check-ins or prayer support can sustain connection without interfering with clinical treatment. Consistency strengthens trust.

Clergy must remain mindful not to replace professional care or revisit therapeutic content. Continued pastoral presence focuses on spiritual encouragement and relational support. This balance honors both roles.

Recognizing Personal Limitations and Seeking Consultation

When uncertainty arises, consultation with supervisors or mental health professionals can provide guidance. Seeking support reflects wisdom, not weakness, and helps clergy maintain effectiveness and well-being.

Consultation offers perspective and accountability. It allows clergy to reflect on complex situations without carrying them alone. This practice supports ethical discernment and emotional sustainability.

Normalizing consultation also models healthy leadership. When clergy seek guidance, they reinforce that support is a strength. This posture protects both the leader and the congregation.

Clergy also carry an ethical responsibility to recognize when a situation extends beyond their scope of practice. In many ministry contexts, pastors are expected to function as all-purpose problem solvers—serving at times as social workers, administrators, maintenance personnel, mediators, counselors, and crisis responders. This reality often fosters a ministry culture of improvisation, where leaders adopt a "we'll figure it out as we go" mentality in order to meet constant and varied demands.

While adaptive problem-solving is often necessary in practical ministry settings, this approach is not appropriate when addressing mental health concerns. Emotional and psychological distress requires informed discernment, ethical restraint, and, at times, specialized intervention. Attempting to manage mental health issues without appropriate training places both the congregant and the clergy member at risk. Ethical pastoral care requires knowing not only how to respond with compassion, but also when to pause, seek guidance, and refer to qualified professionals.

Recognizing limits is not a failure of calling or commitment—it is an expression of responsible leadership. When clergy acknowledge that mental health care cannot be approached through trial and error, they protect the dignity, safety, and well-being of those they serve. Ethical clarity around scope of practice allows clergy to remain faithful to their pastoral role while ensuring congregants receive the level of care their situation requires.

Ethical Awareness in Referral Practices

Ethical pastoral care includes avoiding dual relationships, respecting autonomy, and acting in the best interest of the individual. Ethical discernment supports integrity and trust throughout the referral process.

Ethical awareness helps clergy navigate power dynamics responsibly. Congregants often place significant trust in pastoral authority, making ethical clarity essential. Protecting autonomy ensures that referrals remain supportive rather than coercive.

Ethical referral practices also safeguard long-term relationships. When decisions are guided by integrity rather than convenience or fear, trust is preserved. Ethical consistency strengthens the credibility of pastoral care.

Practice Scenario: Disclosure of Substance Use

A congregant, Jordan, comes to you privately and shares that they are using drugs. Jordan expresses guilt and anxiety and tells you their spouse is unaware of the situation. They are unsure what to do next and are seeking guidance.

Consider the following:

- What factors help you discern whether referral is appropriate at this stage?
- How do confidentiality and pastoral boundaries shape your response?
- What questions would help clarify Jordan's needs without interrogating or advising prematurely?
- How might you normalize professional support while maintaining pastoral care?
- What follow-up support could you offer after discussing referral options?

This scenario may be used for group discussion or individual reflection.

Module 5 Reflection

Before moving forward, take a few moments to reflect and record your thoughts.

What signs most often prompt you to consider referral?

How comfortable are you initiating referral conversations?

What resources are currently available within your community?

Section Review

Before continuing, reflect on your learning in this section.

What information in this section was familiar or already known to you?

What new information or insights did you gain from this section?

The next module focuses on recognizing and responding to mental health crises, equipping clergy to prioritize safety and take appropriate action during urgent situations.

Module 6: Crisis Awareness and Immediate Response

Module Overview

At times, pastoral conversations move beyond ongoing distress into moments of acute crisis. In these situations, clergy are called to respond with clarity, calm, and decisive care. This module focuses on crisis awareness and immediate response, equipping clergy to recognize urgent risk, prioritize safety, and take appropriate action without assuming clinical responsibility. The goal is not to resolve the crisis, but to stabilize the situation and connect individuals with immediate support.

Learning Objectives

By the end of this module, participants will be able to:

- Recognize signs that indicate a mental health crisis
- Assess immediate safety concerns without conducting a clinical evaluation
- Respond calmly and supportively during high-stress situations
- Identify when emergency services or crisis resources are required
- Maintain ethical and pastoral boundaries while prioritizing safety

Understanding Mental Health Crisis

A mental health crisis occurs when an individual's emotional or psychological state presents an immediate risk to themselves or others, or when their ability to function is severely impaired. Crises may involve suicidal ideation, self-harm, threats of violence, extreme agitation, or complete emotional overwhelm. These situations require a shift from supportive pastoral care to urgent, safety-focused action.

Crisis situations differ from ongoing emotional distress in both urgency and risk. While many pastoral conversations involve listening, reflection, and discernment over time, crisis moments require immediate attention to safety. The goal shifts from processing meaning to stabilizing the situation and preventing harm.

Recognizing a crisis early allows clergy to respond responsibly rather than reactively. Clear understanding of what constitutes a mental health crisis helps leaders move decisively without confusion or delay. In these moments, pastoral presence remains important, but it must be paired with action that prioritizes protection and care.

Recognizing Signs of Immediate Risk

Clergy should be attentive to indicators that suggest increased urgency, including:

- Statements about wanting to die or harm oneself
- Expressions of hopelessness combined with intent or planning
- Threats toward others
- Severe disorientation, paranoia, or loss of contact with reality
- Escalating substance use accompanied by impaired judgment

When these signs are present, safety becomes the primary concern.

These indicators should be taken seriously even when they are shared indirectly or casually. Comments made in passing, through humor, or framed spiritually may still signal significant risk. Clergy should trust their instincts when something feels concerning rather than waiting for certainty.

Patterns and escalation matter more than isolated statements. Repeated expressions of despair, increasing agitation, or sudden behavioral changes often indicate that distress is intensifying. Recognizing these signs allows clergy to intervene early and responsibly.

Staying Grounded and Calm

In crisis situations, a clergy member's presence can either escalate or stabilize the moment. Remaining calm, speaking slowly, and maintaining a steady tone helps regulate emotional intensity. A grounded presence communicates safety and reassurance, even when answers are not immediately available.

Clergy may feel internal pressure to act quickly or say the "right" thing. However, emotional regulation begins with the caregiver. When clergy remain steady, they model calm and help reduce panic or fear in the individual experiencing crisis.

Grounded presence does not require certainty or expertise. It requires attentiveness, patience, and emotional containment. Simply being calm and present can significantly reduce escalation and support safer outcomes.

Listening and De-Escalation

During a crisis, listening is more important than explaining. Clergy should allow the individual to express distress without interruption, judgment, or correction. Simple, clear language and nonthreatening body posture support de-escalation. Avoid arguing, minimizing the experience, or attempting to spiritually interpret the crisis in the moment.

Attempts to explain, fix, or reframe during crisis can increase distress. Individuals in crisis often feel overwhelmed and misunderstood. Listening communicates respect and helps reduce emotional intensity.

De-escalation focuses on slowing the interaction rather than resolving the issue. Gentle acknowledgment, brief reassurance, and physical calm help the individual regain a sense of control. This creates space for appropriate next steps.

Assessing Safety Without Diagnosing

Clergy are not responsible for diagnosing mental health conditions, but they are responsible for recognizing when safety may be compromised. Asking direct, compassionate questions—such as whether the individual feels safe or has thoughts of harming themselves—does not increase risk. It clarifies next steps and communicates care.

Many clergy hesitate to ask direct questions out of fear of making the situation worse. Research and best practice consistently show that asking about safety does not plant ideas or increase risk. Instead, it opens the door for honesty.

Clear questions help clergy determine whether immediate intervention is required. Assessing safety supports responsible action while remaining firmly within the pastoral role.

Taking Immediate Action

When there is imminent risk, clergy must act decisively. This may include contacting emergency services, connecting the individual to crisis hotlines, or involving trusted support. In urgent situations, safety overrides confidentiality. Acting promptly is an expression of pastoral responsibility, not failure.

Delaying action in the hope that the situation will improve can increase risk. Clergy should prioritize protection over discomfort or fear of overreacting. Acting decisively demonstrates care and leadership.

Clear documentation of actions taken supports accountability and continuity of care. Immediate action protects lives and reinforces the seriousness of the situation.

How to Use the Pastoral Response Continuum

This visual diagram illustrates the progression of pastoral response as emotional distress intensifies, moving from calm support to emergency action. It is not intended to function as a diagnostic tool, but as a guide to help clergy discern appropriate responses based on observed risk and safety concerns. As an individual's level of distress increases, the pastoral role shifts accordingly—from listening and support, to safety assessment, to decisive intervention.

Clergy should use this continuum to remain proportionate and intentional in their response. Not every situation requires emergency action, but situations that reach imminent risk require immediate steps that prioritize safety over comfort or routine pastoral practice. The diagram reinforces that acting decisively at higher levels of risk is an expression of care and responsibility, not overreaction or failure. Used thoughtfully, this visual supports clarity, confidence, and ethical decision-making during emotionally charged moments.

From Calm Support to Emergency Action

Creating a Safer Environment

When possible, clergy can help reduce immediate risk by ensuring the environment is calm, private, and free from potential harm. Staying with the individual until additional support arrives may be appropriate, provided personal safety is maintained.

Small environmental adjustments can have a meaningful impact during crisis by lowering sensory and emotional overload. Reducing noise, minimizing interruptions, and limiting the number of people present can help stabilize emotional intensity. Creating physical space—such as sitting at eye level, allowing for personal distance, and avoiding closed-off positioning—can support a sense of control and safety for the individual in distress. These adjustments do not resolve the crisis, but they help prevent further escalation while appropriate next steps are taken.

Clergy must also remain mindful of their own safety and limitations. Creating a safer environment includes recognizing when a situation exceeds what can be managed alone and when additional support is required. This may involve involving another trusted leader, contacting emergency services, or stepping away if the environment becomes unsafe. Protecting personal safety is not abandonment; it is a necessary component of responsible pastoral care.

Documentation and Accountability

Following a crisis situation, clergy should document relevant details, including observations, actions taken, and referrals made. Documentation supports continuity of care, accountability, and personal clarity. Records should be handled with discretion and stored securely.

Documentation helps clergy accurately recall what occurred during emotionally intense situations, where memory can be affected by stress or urgency. Recording key observations, timelines, and decisions supports appropriate follow-up and informed consultation with supervisors or professionals if questions arise. Clear documentation also reduces the emotional burden of second-guessing by providing an objective account of actions taken.

Accountability is strengthened when records are maintained consistently and ethically. Documentation allows clergy to reflect on their responses, identify learning opportunities, and ensure alignment with ethical and legal responsibilities. When handled properly, records protect both the congregant and the clergy member and contribute to more informed, responsible ministry practice over time.

Caring for the Caregiver

Responding to crises can be emotionally taxing. Clergy should seek support through supervision, peer consultation, or professional care following crisis situations. Attending to one's own emotional well-being is essential for sustainable ministry.

Exposure to crisis can accumulate gradually, even when individual situations appear resolved. Repeated encounters with trauma, fear, or high-risk situations may lead to emotional exhaustion, compassion fatigue, or diminished clarity. Without intentional processing and support, clergy may carry unresolved emotional weight that affects both personal well-being and ministry effectiveness.

Seeking support after crisis is not optional self-care—it is responsible leadership. When clergy attend to their own emotional health, they model sustainability and wisdom for their congregations. Caring for oneself allows leaders to remain present, grounded, and compassionate over the long term rather than operating from depletion or detachment.

Practice Scenario: Disclosure of Domestic Abuse

A congregant, Jamie, comes to you visibly distressed and shares that they are being abused by their spouse. Jamie expresses fear for their safety and is unsure what steps to take next.

Consider the following:

- What indicators suggest this situation may involve immediate risk?
- What is your primary responsibility in this moment?
- What questions would help you assess safety without conducting an investigation?
- What actions may be necessary to prioritize Jamie's safety?
- How do you remain supportive while recognizing the limits of your role?

This scenario reflects a situation where emotional distress intersects with immediate safety concerns. Domestic abuse often involves fear, secrecy, and confusion, and disclosure may occur only after significant internal struggle. Congregants may feel conflicted, ashamed, or uncertain about what seeking help may require of them emotionally, relationally, or practically. These dynamics make pastoral response especially sensitive and time-critical.

Clergy must remain calm, attentive, and focused on safety while resisting the urge to investigate, mediate, or resolve the situation. The primary responsibility is protection, not problem-solving. Pastoral care in these moments involves listening, affirming the seriousness of the situation, and taking appropriate steps to support safety through referral and external resources when necessary.

This scenario may be used for group discussion or individual reflection.

Module 6 Reflection

Before moving forward, take a few moments to reflect and record your thoughts.

How do you typically respond when situations feel urgent or overwhelming?

What helps you remain calm under pressure?

What crisis and emergency resources are available in your local community?

Section Review

Before continuing, reflect on your learning in this section.

What information in this section was familiar or already known to you?

What new information or insights did you gain from this section?

The next module emphasizes clergy self-care, burnout awareness, and sustainable practices that support long-term ministry health.

Module 7: Clergy Self-Care, Burnout, and Sustainability

Module Overview

Clergy are often called to provide care, leadership, and spiritual stability while navigating ongoing emotional demands. Over time, these responsibilities can contribute to stress, burnout, and isolation if personal well-being is neglected. This module emphasizes clergy self-care as an ethical and pastoral responsibility, equipping ministry leaders to recognize signs of burnout, establish sustainable practices, and seek support without guilt or shame. Caring for oneself is not separate from ministry—it is essential to sustaining it.

Learning Objectives

By the end of this module, participants will be able to:

- Identify common signs of burnout and compassion fatigue in clergy
- Understand how prolonged stress impacts emotional, physical, and spiritual health
- Recognize self-care as a vital component of effective pastoral leadership
- Develop sustainable practices that support long-term ministry health
- Normalize help-seeking and peer support within ministry contexts

Understanding Clergy Burnout

Burnout is a state of emotional, physical, and spiritual exhaustion resulting from prolonged stress and overextension. In ministry, burnout may develop gradually and remain unrecognized due to cultural expectations of constant availability, sacrifice, and resilience. When left unaddressed, burnout can affect judgment, relationships, spiritual vitality, and overall effectiveness in ministry.

Unlike short-term fatigue, burnout accumulates over time and often hides behind faithfulness, productivity, and service. Clergy may continue preaching, leading, and caring for others while privately feeling depleted, disconnected, or overwhelmed. Because ministry frequently rewards endurance and self-sacrifice, warning signs are often spiritualized or ignored rather than addressed.

Burnout does not mean a loss of calling or commitment. It reflects a mismatch between sustained demands and available capacity. Naming burnout honestly allows clergy to move from silent survival toward intentional restoration without fear or self-condemnation.

Common Signs of Burnout and Compassion Fatigue

Clergy experiencing burnout or compassion fatigue may notice:

- Persistent exhaustion or emotional numbness
- Irritability, cynicism, or withdrawal from others
- Difficulty concentrating or making decisions
- Reduced sense of purpose or joy in ministry
- Physical symptoms such as sleep disruption or chronic fatigue

Early recognition allows for intervention before deeper harm occurs.

These signs often emerge subtly and may be dismissed as temporary stress, busy seasons, or spiritual struggle. Over time, however, the accumulation of emotional labor, crisis response, and unmet personal needs can lead to disengagement and emotional flattening. Compassion fatigue may result in feeling detached from congregants or overwhelmed by ongoing needs.

Recognizing these signs requires honesty and self-awareness. Because clergy are accustomed to caring for others, they may minimize their own symptoms or delay seeking support. Early acknowledgment creates space for healing before burnout becomes crisis.

The Cost of Ignoring Self-Care

Neglecting personal well-being can lead to impaired judgment, weakened boundaries, strained relationships, and increased vulnerability to emotional and spiritual distress. Sustainable ministry requires acknowledging personal limits and responding to them with wisdom and care.

When burnout is ignored, clergy may operate on autopilot—functioning outwardly while becoming disconnected inwardly. This can lead to increased reactivity, diminished empathy, or ethical blind spots. Over time, the cost of neglect is often paid by families, congregations, and the clergy themselves.

Ignoring self-care does not strengthen ministry; it erodes it. Faithful leadership includes recognizing when continued depletion threatens both personal health and the integrity of ministry. Responding early preserves calling rather than endangering it.

Self-Care as a Pastoral Responsibility

Self-care is not a departure from calling—it is part of faithful stewardship. Healthy ministry includes rest, reflection, connection, and accountability. When clergy model balanced care, they foster healthier church cultures and reduce stigma around mental health for themselves and others.

Ministry culture often frames self-care as optional or secondary, especially when needs are urgent. However, stewardship of one's emotional, physical, and spiritual health is inseparable from leadership responsibility. Self-care supports clarity, discernment, and sustainable presence.

When clergy prioritize healthy rhythms, they give permission for others to do the same. Modeling balance communicates that well-being and faithfulness are not in competition, but deeply connected.

Establishing Sustainable Practices

Sustainable ministry is supported by practices such as:

- Maintaining clear boundaries around time, availability, and expectations
- Seeking peer support, supervision, or mentoring
- Engaging in spiritual practices that restore rather than deplete
- Attending to physical health, rest, and emotional recovery

Consistency matters more than intensity when building sustainable rhythms.

Sustainable practices are not quick fixes or one-time adjustments. They require ongoing attention and willingness to reassess expectations as ministry contexts change. Small, consistent choices often have greater long-term impact than dramatic but unsustainable efforts.

Building sustainable rhythms also involves resisting comparison and unrealistic standards. Each ministry context carries unique demands, and sustainability looks different across seasons. The goal is not perfection, but responsiveness to what supports long-term faithfulness.

Seeking Support Without Shame

Many clergy hesitate to seek help due to fear of judgment or perceived failure. Normalizing counseling, spiritual direction, and peer support strengthens ministry rather than undermines it. Seeking help is an act of wisdom, humility, and faithfulness.

Shame often keeps clergy isolated even when distress is evident. Concerns about credibility, job security, or congregational perception can delay seeking care. These fears are understandable, but isolation increases risk and prolongs suffering.

Seeking support reflects trust in God's provision through community and professional care. When clergy engage support early, they protect both themselves and those they serve. Support is not a sign of weakness—it is a commitment to longevity and integrity in ministry.

Practice Scenario: Recognizing Burnout

You notice increased irritability, emotional exhaustion, and disengagement in your own ministry work. Tasks that once felt meaningful now feel burdensome, and rest no longer seems restorative.

This scenario reflects common early indicators of burnout that are often dismissed or spiritualized. The gradual loss of joy and effectiveness may feel confusing or discouraging,

Consider the following:

- What signs suggest burnout may be present?
- What internal or external pressures may make these signs easy to dismiss?
- What steps could support restoration and long-term sustainability?

This scenario may be used for group discussion or individual reflection.

Module 7 Reflection

Before moving forward, take a few moments to reflect and record your thoughts.

What practices currently support your well-being?

Where might boundaries need to be strengthened or clarified?

Who are trusted supports you can turn to when ministry becomes overwhelming?

Section Review

Before continuing, reflect on your learning in this section.

What information in this section was familiar or already known to you?

What new information or insights did you gain from this section?

The next module explores cultural awareness and sensitivity in mental health care, helping clergy respond thoughtfully to diverse experiences, backgrounds, and perspectives.

Module 8: Cultural Awareness and Sensitivity in Mental Health Care

Module Overview

Mental health experiences are shaped by culture, background, identity, and community norms. Clergy serve individuals from diverse cultural and social contexts, each influencing how distress is understood, expressed, and addressed. This module focuses on developing cultural awareness and sensitivity in pastoral mental health care, equipping clergy to respond thoughtfully without assumptions, stereotypes, or one-size-fits-all approaches.

Learning Objectives

By the end of this module, participants will be able to:

- Understand how culture influences perceptions of mental health and help-seeking
- Recognize the impact of cultural identity on emotional expression and coping
- Respond to mental health concerns with humility, curiosity, and respect
- Avoid assumptions that may unintentionally harm or marginalize individuals
- Support culturally responsive pastoral care and referral practices

Understanding Culture and Mental Health

Culture shapes how individuals define wellness, distress, resilience, and healing. Beliefs about mental health may be influenced by family systems, faith traditions, ethnicity, socioeconomic background, and community expectations. Awareness of these influences helps clergy respond with sensitivity rather than interpretation or correction.

Cultural frameworks often determine how distress is understood and expressed long before an individual enters a pastoral conversation. What one person names as anxiety or depression, another may describe as stress, spiritual struggle, or physical discomfort. Clergy awareness of these differing frameworks helps prevent misinterpretation and supports more accurate pastoral response.

Understanding culture also requires recognizing one's own cultural lens. Clergy bring personal experiences, assumptions, and norms into every interaction. Reflecting on these influences allows leaders to respond with greater humility and openness, reducing the risk of imposing unintended judgments or expectations.

Cultural Differences in Help-Seeking

Not all individuals view counseling, medication, or professional mental health care in the same way. Cultural stigma, mistrust of systems, past experiences, or spiritual beliefs may affect willingness to seek help. Clergy should approach these differences with openness, recognizing that hesitation does not equal resistance or lack of insight.

In some cultures, seeking outside help may be viewed as a failure of family responsibility or personal strength. Others may have experienced discrimination, misdiagnosis, or lack of culturally competent care, leading to understandable hesitation. These experiences shape how individuals approach mental health resources.

Clergy support begins with listening rather than persuasion. By acknowledging concerns and validating hesitation, leaders create space for honest conversation. Trust often grows when individuals feel their values are respected rather than challenged.

Communication Across Cultural Contexts

Cultural norms influence how emotions are expressed, discussed, or withheld. Some individuals may communicate distress indirectly or prioritize relational harmony over disclosure. Clergy should listen carefully for meaning beyond words and avoid imposing their own communication expectations onto others.

Silence, storytelling, physical symptoms, or spiritual language may carry significant meaning in certain cultural contexts. What appears as avoidance may actually reflect deeply ingrained communication norms. Attentive listening helps clergy recognize these patterns without rushing interpretation.

Effective pastoral care adapts to the communicator rather than requiring conformity. When clergy adjust pacing, language, and expectations, they create environments where individuals feel safer sharing at their own pace.

Avoiding Assumptions and Stereotypes

Assumptions—whether positive or negative—can undermine trust and care. Cultural humility requires acknowledging what we do not know and remaining open to learning from each individual's lived experience. Asking respectful questions is often more helpful than relying on generalizations.

Even well-intentioned assumptions can create distance. Assuming shared values, beliefs, or experiences may unintentionally silence important differences. Cultural humility invites curiosity rather than certainty.

Clergy demonstrate respect by allowing individuals to define their own experiences. This posture strengthens relationships and supports more effective pastoral discernment. Humility fosters trust, especially in cross-cultural interactions.

Faith, Culture, and Mental Health

Faith traditions intersect with culture in complex ways. Spiritual beliefs may influence how suffering is interpreted, how healing is sought, and who is trusted for support. Clergy must remain attentive to how faith and culture together shape mental health experiences, especially when providing guidance or referrals.

In some contexts, faith may be the primary lens through which all distress is understood. In others, spiritual language may coexist with skepticism toward formal religious structures. These dynamics influence where individuals seek help and how they respond to pastoral care.

Clergy who recognize this intersection avoid simplistic explanations. Respecting both faith and cultural context allows leaders to offer guidance that is spiritually grounded and culturally responsive.

Culturally Responsive Pastoral Care

Culturally responsive care involves adapting pastoral responses to honor an individual's background while maintaining ethical and pastoral boundaries. This may include adjusting language, involving trusted community support, or collaborating with culturally competent mental health professionals.

Responsiveness does not mean abandoning standards or responsibilities. Instead, it involves thoughtful flexibility within ethical limits. Clergy remain attentive to both cultural values and safety considerations.

Collaboration with culturally informed resources strengthens care. When clergy help connect individuals to professionals who understand their cultural context, they reduce barriers and increase the likelihood of effective support.

Practice Scenario: Cultural Sensitivity in Pastoral Care

A congregant shares emotional distress but expresses hesitation about counseling, citing family expectations and cultural beliefs about handling problems privately.

This scenario reflects a common tension between personal distress and cultural expectations. The congregant may fear disappointing family members, violating cultural norms, or being perceived as weak. These concerns deserve careful attention.

Consider the following:

- How might culture be influencing this individual's perspective on mental health care?
- What questions could help you better understand their concerns?
- How can you support them without pressuring or dismissing their values?

This scenario may be used for group discussion or individual reflection.

Module 8 Reflection

Before moving forward, take a few moments to reflect and record your thoughts.

How has your own background shaped your views on mental health?

Where might cultural differences challenge your assumptions?

How can curiosity strengthen your pastoral responses?

Section Review

Before continuing, reflect on your learning in this section.

What information in this section was familiar or already known to you?

What new information or insights did you gain from this section?

The next module addresses legal and ethical considerations in pastoral mental health care, including confidentiality, boundaries, and mandatory reporting responsibilities.

Module 9: Legal and Ethical Considerations in Pastoral Mental Health Care

Module Overview

Pastoral care involves deep trust, vulnerability, and responsibility. When mental health concerns are present, clergy must navigate ethical obligations and legal requirements with wisdom and care. This module provides an overview of key legal and ethical considerations relevant to pastoral mental health care, helping clergy protect congregants, themselves, and the integrity of ministry while remaining faithful to their pastoral role.

Learning Objectives

By the end of this module, participants will be able to:

- Understand the difference between pastoral care and clinical mental health treatment
- Recognize ethical responsibilities related to confidentiality, boundaries, and power dynamics
- Identify situations that require mandatory reporting or immediate action
- Navigate legal considerations without assuming a clinical role
- Practice ethical discernment while supporting congregants' well-being

Pastoral Care vs. Clinical Care

Clergy provide spiritual guidance, emotional support, and pastoral presence, but they do not provide clinical diagnosis or treatment unless formally trained and licensed to do so. Understanding this distinction is essential for ethical ministry. Confusing roles can place congregants at risk and expose clergy to legal and ethical complications.

Pastoral care focuses on spiritual accompaniment, meaning-making, prayer, and relational support, while clinical care addresses assessment, diagnosis, and treatment of mental health conditions. Although these roles may overlap in concern for the individual's well-being, they are not interchangeable. When clergy attempt to function as clinicians without appropriate training, they risk offering care that exceeds their competence and compromises safety.

Clear role distinction protects both the congregant and the clergy member. Congregants benefit from receiving the appropriate level of care for their needs, and clergy are freed to serve confidently within their calling. Ethical ministry requires humility about limits and clarity about responsibility, especially when mental health concerns are present.

Confidentiality and Its Limits

Confidentiality is foundational to trust in pastoral relationships. However, confidentiality is not absolute. Clergy must understand when information cannot remain private, particularly in situations involving imminent harm, abuse, or legal obligations. Clear communication about the limits of confidentiality helps maintain transparency and trust.

Explaining confidentiality early in the pastoral relationship helps prevent misunderstanding during moments of crisis. When congregants understand that safety concerns may require additional action, they are less likely to feel betrayed if limits are reached. Transparency supports trust even when difficult decisions must be made.

Ethical pastoral care balances confidentiality with responsibility. Clergy must prioritize protection over secrecy when safety is at risk. Communicating these boundaries with compassion reinforces integrity and demonstrates that care extends beyond conversation to action when necessary.

Mandatory Reporting Responsibilities

In many jurisdictions, clergy are required to report certain disclosures, such as suspected abuse of children, elders, or vulnerable adults. Laws vary by location and role. Clergy are encouraged to become familiar with local reporting requirements and denominational policies to ensure compliance while responding with compassion.

Mandatory reporting obligations can feel daunting, especially when pastoral relationships are built on trust and care. However, reporting requirements exist to protect vulnerable individuals and prevent further harm. Understanding these obligations before a situation arises helps clergy respond calmly and responsibly.

Clergy should seek guidance from denominational leadership, legal counsel, or professional resources when questions arise about reporting. Acting in accordance with the law and policy does not negate compassion; it reinforces commitment to safety and ethical leadership.

Ethical Boundaries and Power Dynamics

Pastoral relationships inherently involve power differences. Ethical boundaries protect both clergy and congregants from harm. Maintaining appropriate limits around time, availability, emotional reliance, and dual relationships supports healthy ministry and reduces the risk of exploitation or burnout.

Power dynamics are often subtle and unspoken. Congregants may defer to clergy authority or feel pressure to comply with suggestions, even when discomfort exists. Ethical awareness helps clergy remain attentive to how influence operates within pastoral relationships.

Clear boundaries safeguard trust and sustainability. When limits are respected, relationships remain supportive rather than dependent. Ethical boundaries allow clergy to care deeply without crossing into roles or behaviors that compromise integrity or well-being.

Informed Consent and Transparency

Ethical pastoral care includes clarity about role, scope, and expectations. Clergy should be transparent about what pastoral support can and cannot provide, especially when mental health concerns are present. This transparency supports informed decision-making and appropriate referral.

Informed consent in pastoral settings involves ongoing communication rather than a single conversation. Clergy should revisit expectations as situations evolve, ensuring congregants understand the nature and limits of pastoral care. This clarity empowers individuals to make informed choices about their support.

Transparency strengthens trust. When clergy communicate openly, congregants are less likely to feel misled or confused. Ethical clarity creates a foundation for collaboration and referral when additional care is needed.

Documentation and Record-Keeping

When pastoral care involves mental health concerns, brief and factual documentation may be appropriate. Documentation should focus on observations, actions taken, and referrals made— not clinical interpretations. Records should be stored securely and handled with discretion in accordance with church policy and legal guidance.

Documentation provides clarity in situations that may later require reflection or consultation. Recording what was observed and what actions were taken helps clergy maintain accuracy and accountability, particularly in emotionally intense circumstances.

Responsible record-keeping protects both the congregant and the clergy member. Clear, factual notes support continuity of care and ethical practice while respecting privacy and confidentiality requirements.

Consultation and Referral as Ethical Practice

Seeking consultation or making referrals is not a failure of pastoral care—it is an ethical responsibility. Collaboration with mental health professionals, supervisors, or denominational leaders strengthens care and protects all involved. Ethical practice recognizes when additional expertise is needed.

Consultation provides perspective and accountability, especially in complex or high-risk situations. It allows clergy to process concerns without isolation and to confirm that responses align with ethical standards and best practices.

Referral honors the limits of pastoral care while prioritizing congregant well-being. When clergy normalize consultation and referral, they reinforce that ethical leadership values collaboration over self-sufficiency. This approach strengthens ministry integrity and sustainability.

Practice Scenario: Ethical Discernment

A congregant shares ongoing emotional distress and asks you to keep the conversation entirely confidential, even as concerns about safety begin to emerge.

This scenario highlights the tension between trust, confidentiality, and responsibility. Clergy may feel pulled between honoring the congregant's request and responding to potential risk. Ethical discernment requires careful consideration of both relational trust and safety obligations.

Consider the following:

- What ethical principles are at play in this situation?
- How do confidentiality and safety interact here?
- What steps support both ethical responsibility and pastoral care?

This scenario may be used for group discussion or individual reflection.

Module 9 Reflection

Before moving forward, take a few moments to reflect and record your thoughts.

Where do you feel most confident navigating ethical boundaries?

What legal responsibilities are you aware of in your ministry context?

Who can you consult when ethical questions arise?

Section Review

Before continuing, reflect on your learning in this section.

What information in this section was familiar or already known to you?

What new information or insights did you gain from this section?

The final section of this training provides practical resources, references, and tools to support ongoing learning and responsible pastoral care.

Module 10: Evaluation and Participant Feedback

Module Overview

Effective training includes opportunities for reflection, evaluation, and growth. This module focuses on assessing learning outcomes and gathering participant feedback to strengthen understanding, improve future training, and support accountability. Evaluation is not about grading performance, but about identifying growth, confidence, and areas for continued development in pastoral mental health care.

Learning Objectives

By the end of this module, participants will be able to:

- Reflect on personal learning and growth throughout the training
- Identify areas of increased confidence and remaining uncertainty
- Provide constructive feedback on the training experience
- Understand the role of evaluation in professional and pastoral development

Purpose of Evaluation

Evaluation helps ensure that training goals are met and that participants feel equipped to apply what they have learned. For clergy, evaluation also supports self-awareness, ethical practice, and ongoing formation rather than performance-based assessment.

Self-Assessment and Reflection

Self-assessment allows participants to consider how their understanding, attitudes, and confidence have changed. Reflection may include identifying strengths, acknowledging limitations, and recognizing areas for continued learning.

Participant Feedback

Feedback from participants provides valuable insight into the effectiveness of the training content, structure, and delivery. Honest feedback helps refine future training while honoring the lived experiences of those participating.

Using Feedback for Growth

Evaluation findings should be used to support growth rather than criticism. Leaders and facilitators can use feedback to adapt training, provide additional resources, and strengthen support systems for clergy.

Practice Reflection: Training Impact

Consider the following:

- What areas of this training were most helpful for your ministry context?
- Where do you feel more confident than when you began?
- What topics would benefit from additional learning or discussion?

Module 10 Reflection

Before moving forward, take a few moments to reflect and record your thoughts.

How will you continue applying what you have learned?

What support will help you sustain these practices over time?

Section Review

Before continuing, reflect on your learning in this section.

What information in this section was familiar or already known to you?

What new information or insights did you gain from this section?

The final module focuses on follow-up support and peer collaboration, emphasizing the importance of ongoing connection and shared learning in sustainable ministry.

Module 11: Follow-Up Support and Peer Collaboration

Module Overview

Mental health care in ministry is not a one-time effort but an ongoing process. This module emphasizes the importance of follow-up support, peer collaboration, and shared accountability in sustaining healthy pastoral practices. Ongoing connection reduces isolation, reinforces learning, and strengthens clergy resilience over time.

Learning Objectives

By the end of this module, participants will be able to:

- Recognize the value of follow-up support after training
- Identify opportunities for peer collaboration and mutual accountability
- Understand how shared learning supports long-term ministry health
- Commit to continued growth and connection beyond the training setting

The Importance of Follow-Up Support

Training is most effective when followed by continued reflection and support. Follow-up allows clergy to process real-life application, revisit challenges, and strengthen confidence as new situations arise.

Learning does not end when training concludes. As clergy begin applying new frameworks in real ministry contexts, questions and uncertainties naturally emerge. Follow-up support provides space to reflect on these experiences, refine responses, and integrate learning more fully into daily practice.

Continued engagement also helps prevent isolation. When clergy know that support remains available beyond the training environment, they are more likely to approach difficult situations with confidence rather than hesitation.

Peer Collaboration in Ministry

Peer relationships provide encouragement, perspective, and shared wisdom. Collaborating with other clergy reduces isolation and creates spaces for honest conversation, prayer, and mutual support around mental health challenges.

Ministry can be uniquely isolating, especially when navigating complex emotional or ethical situations. Peer collaboration offers reassurance that challenges are shared rather than personal failures. These relationships allow clergy to speak openly in ways that may not feel possible within their own congregations.

Regular connection with trusted peers supports accountability and emotional health. When clergy intentionally cultivate these relationships, they strengthen both personal resilience and ministry effectiveness.

Creating Supportive Networks

Supportive networks may include peer groups, mentoring relationships, denominational cohorts, or interdisciplinary partnerships. These connections help clergy remain grounded, accountable, and supported in their pastoral role.

Networks function best when they are intentional and appropriately structured. Clear expectations around confidentiality, frequency of connection, and purpose help ensure that support remains consistent and meaningful. Diverse networks also allow clergy to draw from a range of perspectives and experiences.

Participation in supportive networks reinforces the message that ministry is not meant to be carried alone. These relationships provide stability during seasons of challenge and encouragement during seasons of growth.

Sustaining Growth Over Time

Sustainable ministry requires ongoing learning and intentional connection. Returning to training materials, seeking consultation, and engaging in peer dialogue reinforce healthy practices and prevent burnout.

Growth is maintained through small, consistent practices rather than dramatic changes. Revisiting key concepts, reflecting on real-life application, and seeking feedback support long-term integration. These rhythms help clergy respond thoughtfully rather than reactively.

Sustaining growth also involves recognizing when additional support is needed. Continued learning and connection ensure that clergy remain responsive to changing ministry demands while protecting their own well-being.

Practice Reflection: Ongoing Support

Consider the following:

- Who are trusted peers you can connect with regularly?
- What structures could support continued collaboration?
- How will you seek support when challenges arise?

This reflection invites intentional planning rather than vague intention. Identifying specific supports and structures increases the likelihood that connection and collaboration will continue beyond the training setting.

Module 11 Reflection

Before concluding, take a few moments to reflect and record your thoughts.

What commitments will you make to ongoing support and collaboration?

How can you contribute to healthier ministry culture within your context?

Section Review

Before continuing, reflect on your learning in this section.

What information in this section was familiar or already known to you?

What new information or insights did you gain from this section?

Glossary

This glossary provides definitions for key terms used throughout the training to support clarity and shared understanding.

Burnout
A state of emotional, physical, and spiritual exhaustion caused by prolonged stress and overextension, often resulting in reduced effectiveness, cynicism, or loss of purpose in ministry.

Clinical Care
Mental health services provided by licensed professionals that may include diagnosis, treatment planning, therapy, or medication management. Clinical care is distinct from pastoral care.

Compassion Fatigue
Emotional and physical depletion that can occur when caregivers are exposed to ongoing suffering, reducing their ability to empathize or remain emotionally present.

Confidentiality
The ethical responsibility to protect private information shared within a pastoral relationship, with recognized limits when safety or legal obligations require disclosure.

Crisis
An acute situation in which an individual's emotional or psychological state presents immediate risk to themselves or others, or significantly impairs functioning and requires urgent intervention.

Cultural Awareness
An understanding of how culture, background, identity, and community norms influence perceptions of mental health, emotional expression, and help-seeking behaviors.

Cultural Humility
An ongoing posture of openness, self-awareness, and willingness to learn from others' lived experiences without assumptions or stereotypes.

Discernment
The thoughtful and prayerful process of recognizing what type of response or support is most appropriate in a given pastoral situation.

Ethical Boundaries
Guidelines that protect both clergy and congregants by defining appropriate limits related to roles, power dynamics, availability, and relationships.

Faith-Based Misconceptions
Inaccurate beliefs that frame mental health concerns as spiritual failure, lack of faith, or moral weakness, often increasing stigma and discouraging help-seeking.

Help-Seeking
The process of reaching out for support, whether through pastoral care, professional mental health services, or community resources.

Mandatory Reporting
Legal requirements that obligate clergy to report certain disclosures, such as suspected abuse or imminent harm, regardless of confidentiality expectations.

Mental Health
A person's emotional, psychological, and social well-being, influencing how they think, feel, act, cope with stress, and relate to others.

Mental Health Conditions
Diagnosable patterns of emotional, cognitive, or behavioral disturbance that significantly affect functioning and may require professional treatment.

Mental Health Literacy
A foundational understanding of mental health concepts that enables clergy to recognize concerns, respond appropriately, and make informed referrals.

Pastoral Care
Spiritual guidance, emotional support, and relational presence provided by clergy within the scope of ministry, distinct from clinical mental health treatment.

Pastoral Boundaries
Limits that help clergy remain supportive without assuming responsibilities beyond their role or training.

Referral
The process of guiding a congregant toward professional mental health services or additional support when pastoral care alone is insufficient.

Self-Care
Intentional practices that support emotional, physical, and spiritual well-being, essential for sustainable ministry and ethical leadership.

Spiritual Struggle
Internal conflict related to faith, doubt, guilt, or meaning that may accompany emotional distress or mental health challenges.

Stigma
Negative beliefs or attitudes about mental health that discourage open conversation and help-seeking.

Trauma
Emotional or psychological injury resulting from distressing or life-threatening experiences that may affect memory, behavior, emotional regulation, and sense of safety.